POEMS BY
ELOISE GREENFIELD

I Can Draw a Weeposaur and Other Dinosaurs

PICTURES BY
JAN SPIVEY GILCHRIST

Greenwillow Books
An Imprint of HarperCollinsPublishers

A black pen, watercolors, and color markers were used for the full-color art.
The text is set in Egyptian 505 and Gill Sans.

Printed in Hong Kong by South China Printing Company (1988) Ltd.
www.harperchildrens.com

Library of Congress Cataloging-in-Publication Data
Greenfield, Eloise.
I can draw a weeposaur / by Eloise Greenfield;
illustrated by Jan Spivey Gilchrist.
p.   cm.
"Greenwillow Books."
Summary: A young girl depicts in poems and drawings
the imaginary dinosaurs that she dreams up, like the sleeposaurus,
the florasaurus, and Mr. and Mrs. Cha-Chasaurus.
ISBN 0-688-17634-8 (trade).   ISBN 0-688-17635-6 (lib. bdg.)
1. Animals, Mythical—Juvenile poetry.   2. Dinosaurs—Juvenile poetry.
3. Children's poetry, American.   [1. Animals, Mythical—Poetry.
2. Dinosaurs—Poetry.   3. American poetry.]
I. Gilchrist, Jan Spivey, ill.   II. Title.
PS3557.R39416I2   2001   811'.54—dc21   99-42419   CIP

1 2 3 4 5 6 7 8 9 10
First Edition

To Kamaria Joyce Greenfield,
our granddaughter and goddaughter,
who inspired us with her drawings
of dinosaurs

—E. G. and J. S. G.

CONTENTS

ARTIST

My head is too small
to hold them all
inside.
"Let us out!"
I hear them say,
so I become my artist self
and set them free.

SPEEDASAURUS

She never speaks to carnivores,
She doesn't stop to play,
She dashes right on by them
When they look the other way.

FLORASAURUS

She eats up all the flowers growing
In her neighborhood,
The neighbors tried to buy her some,
But they weren't half as good.
And so, because she aims to please
(Although it's really hard),
She leaves every single stem
To decorate the yard.

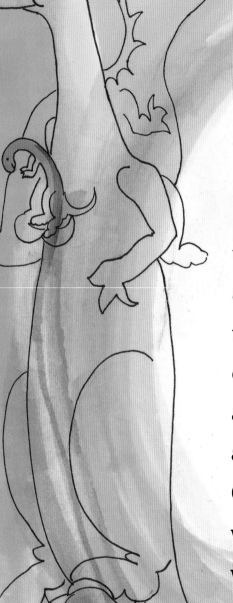

COLORS

I spread the colors

thin and heavy and long

and short,

the shapes come,

curved and straight,

and soon there are feet,

a head, a body.

Oh, I am happy

when I see

what I have done.

TORTOISAURUS

She carries a beautiful home on her back,
A rambler with windows that slide,
But what good's a home, even one that
    can roam,
If you can't get your whole self inside?

SHOPPERSAURUS

He buys boxes of this,
And boxes of that,
The dinosaur mall
Is his main habitat.

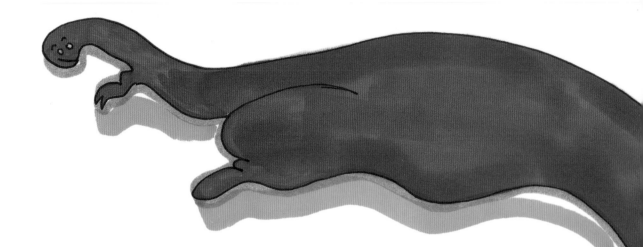

MY DINOSAURS

My dinosaurs
walk from my brush
and live,
they do what my
moving hand
tells them to do,
they are paint
on paper.
I love them.

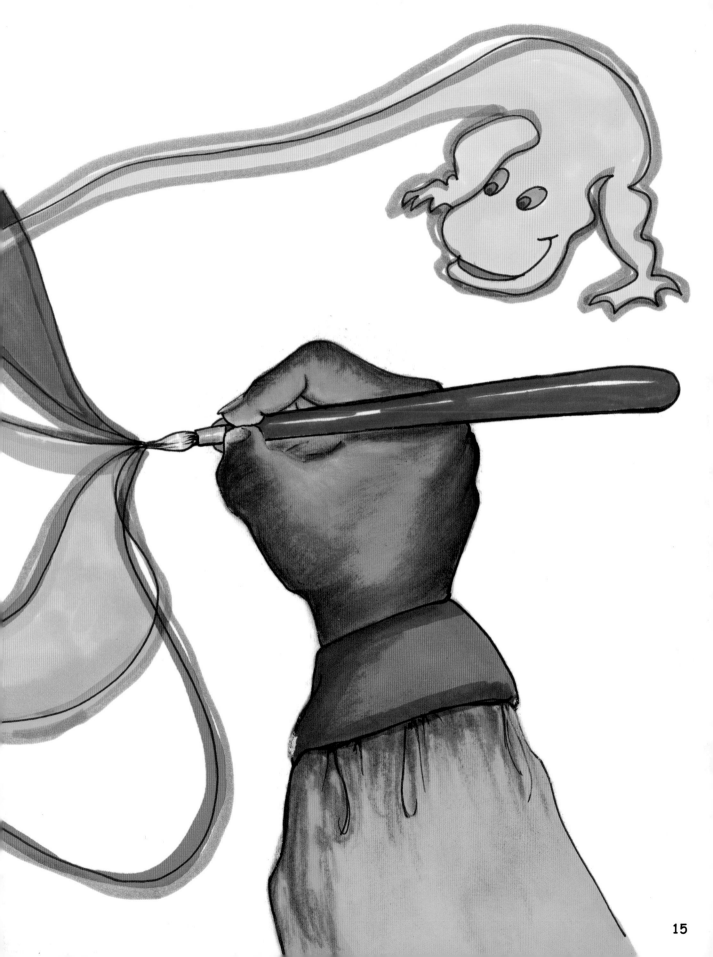

TRICKOSAURUS

He fell when he tried to do a handstand,
He fell when he walked a beam,
But he was the greatest at landing on top
Of his gymnastics team.

BABYSAURUS

He's his mama's little baby,
Smiling sweet in Tennessee,
But his middle's in Montana,
And his tail's in Waikiki.

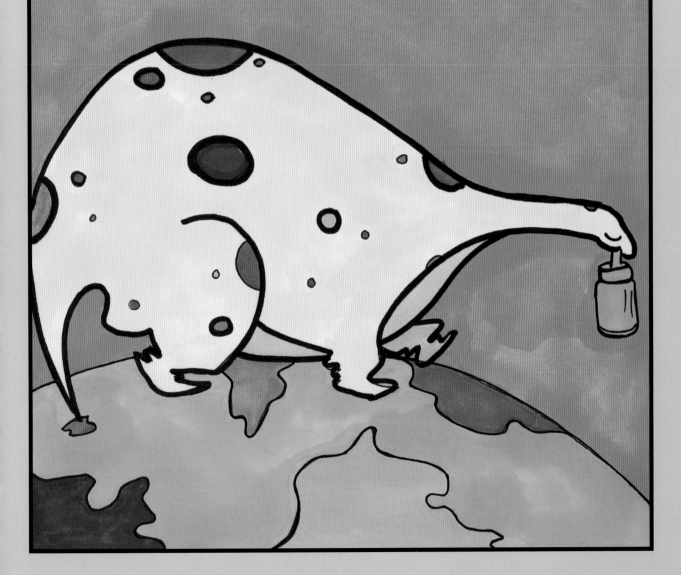

LAUGHTER

I don't even smile
till the picture is done,
then I laugh,
have to laugh,
can't help it because
my dinosaurs have forgotten
where they came from,
but I remember.

WEEPOSAURUS

He cries for joy and sadness,
His crying has no end,
He bawls and hollers all night long
To wake up his best friend.

SLEEPOSAURUS

The sound of loud weeping wakes him,
He opens one eye for a peek,
How cruel of Weepo to shake him awake
When he's only slept for a week.

SINGERSAURUS

When they ask him to sing,
He is bashful.
His chest caves in,
He drops his head,
His voice is only a whisper.

But when he's alone,
He's a great baritone,
He throws his head back,
And his voice is loud.
"I am the king of singers!"
        he sings,
And the audience hiding
Behind the hills
Is happy.

MY FRIEND

She doesn't know
I know that she
is poking fun at me.
I let her have her fun,
I crack up at her jokes,
I draw funny dinosaurs,
and she draws funny
folks.

SMELLASAURUS

She makes her own perfume,
She takes four bottles from the shelf,
She pours the bottles on herself,
So she can be the sweetest girl
        around,
But all the girls who smell like roses
Clap their hands up to their noses,
Screaming, "Oh, no! Smella's back
        in town!"

MR. AND MRS. CHA-CHASAURUS

In her gown and his tuxedo,
They cha-cha with charm and grace,
And it matters not a bit
That she has never seen his face.

MESSYSAURUS

What in the world
        is wrong with her room?
Her room is extremely rude,
She turns her back, and it fills itself
With toys and games and food.
It deserves to be dirty forever,
Or taken to court and sued,
Well, she's not going to clean it up
        ever again,
She's just not in the mood!

MY ROOM IS FULL

My room is full,
but my hand won't stop,
won't stop,
putting paint on paper,
paint on paper,
paint . . .

ELOISE GREENFIELD's name is a household word wherever children read poetry. The prize-winning author of more than thirty-eight books, Ms. Greenfield grew up in Washington, D.C. She is the mother of a son and a daughter and the grandmother of four. Among her most popular books are *Honey, I Love*, an ALA Notable Book; *Africa Dream*, winner of the Coretta Scott King Award; and *Rosa Parks*, winner of the first Carter G. Woodson Award. She lives in Washington, D.C.

JAN SPIVEY GILCHRIST was born and grew up in Chicago. Like the child in this book, she says she has been an artist for as long as she can remember. She received a Masters degree in painting from the University of Northern Iowa. Among her best-loved picture books are *Nathaniel Talking* by Eloise Greenfield, which won the Coretta Scott King Award for art, and *Night On Neighborhood Street*, also by Eloise Greenfield, which won a Coretta Scott King Honor for both art and text. She and her husband and son, William, live in Chicago.